# LITTLE LIBRARY

# In Greek Times

## Christopher Maynard

Kingfisher Books

# Contents

# In the beginning...

Just under 3,000 years ago, a number of small Greek cities began to grow in size and power. The people who lived in the cities made marvellous buildings and created beautiful works of art. They developed new ideas about art, science and government, and little by little their ideas spread – at first to Mediterranean countries, and then beyond.

# A land of cities

G reece is very mountainous. Its cities were like small countries or states, cut off from their neighbours by rugged mountain ranges.

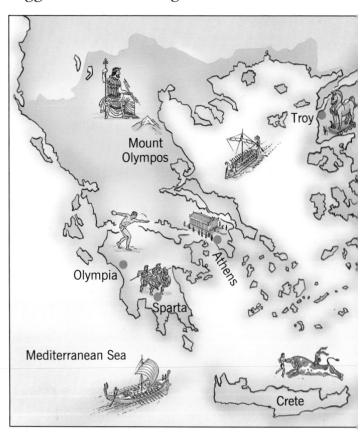

Troy

Mount Olympos

Olympia

Sparta

Athens

Mediterranean Sea

Crete

In earliest times, each city was ruled by a king, or one or more powerful men. Later, in some cities, all the freemen shared in running the government. This is called democracy. The Greeks were the first people to practise it.

KEY

☐ Greek lands

Ephesus

Greece

▽ Alexander the Great and his father, King Philip of Macedon, were the first people to try to rule over all the Greek city-states, about 2,300 years ago.

# Going to war

Fighting often broke out between the city-states. The most powerful ones, Athens and Sparta, went to war many times. The Spartans had a full-time army, but the other cities only called their freemen to arms when a war started.

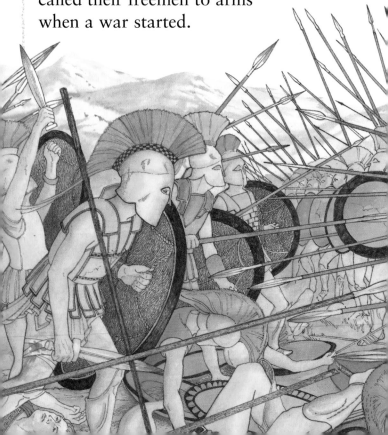

Greek foot soldiers were called hoplites. They fought shoulder to shoulder, in closely packed lines known as phalanxes. In battle, enemy phalanxes tried to smash through each other's line.

# Ships and the sea

Travelling by ship was far quicker than scaling mountains, so long journeys were usually made by sea. Cargoes of oil, wheat and wine were carried in tubby merchant ships. But merchant ships sailed slowly and were easily captured by pirates.

Fast Athenian warships were built to protect traders. Fleets of these long narrow vessels patrolled the eastern Mediterranean. Out at sea, they cruised under sail. Coming into harbour, or in an attack, they were rowed. A ram at the front was used to sink enemies.

# Athens

The largest and most splendid of the Greek city-states was Athens. It is the capital of Greece today, and many of its ancient buildings are still standing.

The city was named after its patron goddess, Athena. It grew up round an acropolis. This was once a hill-top fort, but later it became a holy place with beautiful temples, such as the Parthenon. You can see the acropolis hill at the top of the picture.

---

### KEY TO ATHENS

① Parthenon, the main temple of the goddess Athena
② Statue of Athena
③ Gateway to the acropolis
④ Temple of Athena Victorious
⑤ Agora, the market place

# Make a temple

T he Parthenon temple was built
2,500 years ago for Athena, the
goddess of war and wisdom.

You'll need a sheet of
tracing paper, a ruler and
a pencil, some thin card,
felt-tip pens or crayons, a
pair of scissors and some
glue.

**1** Copy this plan on to
the tracing paper, then
make it bigger using a
photocopying machine.
**2** Stick the copy on card
and cut around the solid
black lines.

Flap

**A**

**B**

**3** Colour your temple in. The real Parthenon was made of glistening white marble, and had statues and brightly coloured paintings between the roof and the columns supporting it.

**4** Fold the card inwards along the dotted lines, then glue in the flaps to hold the temple together. Glue the roof flaps first (A), then the side ones (B).

Flap

# Living in a town

There was no roar of traffic in the middle of a Greek town. All the noise came from people and animals.

Narrow streets bustled with people from dawn to dusk. Since towns were built on hills, the streets were often quite steep. They were lined with shops and houses, which were built from mud-bricks and then white-washed.

People shopped with gold or silver coins, like this 4-drachma piece. Each city made its own coins and put a symbol on them. Athenian coins were stamped with an owl, the sign of the goddess Athena.

### GOING SHOPPING

Women ran the household and looked after the money, but shopping was usually men's work. Instead of using a purse, they often carried small coins in their mouths.

# Inside a home

Houses were usually built around an open courtyard. In the middle was an altar, where the family prayed.

Women and men had separate living rooms, and never ate together if there were guests. The meals were cooked by wives and daughters or, in wealthy homes, female servants. The men of the house lay on couches, eating from a low table.

KEY TO HOUSE

① Entrance to the house
② Food was stored in sacks and pots
③ Women's room, for cloth-making
④ Bedroom, with low wooden beds
⑤ The men's sitting room
⑥ Bathroom
⑦ Kitchen, with charcoal cooking fire
⑧ Men had their own dining room
⑨ Sometimes a room was let as a shop

As well as cooking all the meals, women were kept busy spinning and weaving cloth, and making clothes for the family. There were no cupboards to put the clothes in – they were stored in wooden chests.

# Going to school

Only the sons of freemen went to school in Ancient Greece. Girls were taught by their mothers. Lessons had to be paid for, so boys from poor families probably left school early.

Starting when they were six or seven, boys were taught to read, write, dance and play music. Lots of time was also spent doing athletics.

Children wrote by scratching with a stick called a stylus into a wax tablet. Mistakes were easily rubbed out!

### HOME WORK

Girls were taught weaving, and all the other skills they needed to run a household, by their mothers.

# At the theatre

The Greeks were the first people to build theatres. Their plays grew out of songs and dances performed for Dionysos, the god of wine. The actors were all men, wearing masks painted to show the character they were playing.

# MAKE A GREEK MASK

You'll need a sheet of thin card, some scissors, felt-tip pens, glue and sticky tape, a stick and some thick knitting wool.

**1** Draw a face shape with two big eye holes on to the card. Cut around it, and inside the eye holes.

**2** Paint a sad face with the mouth turned down on one side of the card, and a happy smiling face on the other side.

**3** Glue and tape the stick firmly below the mouth, as a handle.
**4** Paint glue around the bottom of the sad mask, then stick on wool to make a beard. When it's dry, turn the mask round and do the same with the happy side.

23

# Storytelling

**P**eople in Greece loved listening to stories about their gods and heroes. Even today we still enjoy tales from two great Ancient Greek poems, the *Iliad* and the *Odyssey*. The poems describe the war between the Greeks and the city of Troy, as well as the victorious Greek warriors' long journey home, and all their amazing adventures.

The *Iliad* and *Odyssey* tell us much about Greek legends and history. The Trojan War is said to have ended after the people of Troy were tricked into letting enemy soldiers hiding inside a wooden horse into their city.

People used to think both poems were written by one man, Homer. It is more likely that over hundreds of years, many poets told and retold the stories.

# Greek gods

The Greeks believed in a big family of gods and goddesses. The heads of the whole family were the king and queen of the gods, Zeus and his wife Hera. They lived with all the other gods in a land above the clouds over Mount Olympos, the highest mountain peak in Greece.

Temples were the gods' homes. There was often a statue of the god inside.

# WHO AM I?

Each god or goddess controlled different things on Earth – from the seas and oceans, to music and poetry. Some of their names and jobs are listed below. Can you match the gods and goddesses with their pictures? (The answers are on page 30.)

① **Athena**
Goddess of war and wisdom

② **Ares**
God of war

③ **Aphrodite**
Goddess of love and beauty

④ **Poseidon**
God of the sea

⑤ **Zeus**
King of the gods

⑥ **Demeter**
Goddess of farming and the harvest

⑦ **Artemis**
Goddess of hunting

⑧ **Apollo**
God of music

# Olympic Games

T he very first Olympic Games were
held nearly 2,800 years ago, as
part of a festival for Zeus. They took
place at a town called Olympia, where
there was a special temple for the god.

The Games lasted for five days, and
they were held every four years. All of
the athletes were men. Women could
take part in separate games
during a festival for the
goddess Hera.

Male athletes didn't wear
any clothes – one reason
why women couldn't take
part in the same games as
them. This man is about to
throw a discus. You can still
watch discus-throwers at
athletics meetings today.
The first modern Olympic
Games were held in 1896.

# HOST YOUR OWN OLYMPICS

Try holding your own games at school or in the local park. You'll need lots of space, a long tape measure, and a piece of chalk to mark starting and finishing lines, and distances jumped or thrown.

## 1 Hundred-metre-dash
Compare your time with the world record – ask for help in the library to look this up in a book.

## 2 Long jump
Greek athletes used to carry a weight in each hand. Try making your jump without a weight, then do it carrying something in each hand!

## 3 Discus throwing
Make sure there aren't any windows nearby. Throw a plastic plate or a frisbee.

The winning Greek athlete was given a crown of leaves. Make your own by cutting leaf-shapes from green paper, and stapling them to a head-sized piece of knotted elastic.

# Index

③ ⑦ ⑥ ②

④ ⑧ ⑤ ①